STONY CREEK LIBRARY
1350 GREENFIELD PIKE
NOBLESVILLE, IN 46060

HOLIDAY ORIGAMI

Independence Day Origami

by Ruth Owen

PowerKiDS
press

New York

Published in 2013 by The Rosen Publishing Group, Inc.
29 East 21st Street, New York, NY 10010

Copyright © 2013 by The Rosen Publishing Group, Inc.

All rights reserved. No part of this book may be reproduced in any form without permission in writing from the publisher, except by a reviewer.

Produced for Rosen by Ruby Tuesday Books Ltd
Editor for Ruby Tuesday Books Ltd: Mark J. Sachner
US Editor: Sara Antill
Designer: Emma Randall

Photo Credits:
Cover, 1, 3, 4 (top), 5, 7 (top), 7 (center), 8, 12, 13 (top right), 16, 20, 24, 25 (top center), 28, 29 (top right) © Shutterstock; 7 (bottom) © Emre Ayaroglu, Creative Commons Wikipedia. Origami models © Ruby Tuesday Books Ltd.

Library of Congress Cataloging-in-Publication Data

Owen, Ruth, 1967–
 Independence Day origami / by Ruth Owen.
      p. cm. — (Holiday origami)
 Includes index.
 ISBN 978-1-4488-7863-5 (library binding) — ISBN 978-1-4488-7922-9 (pbk.) — ISBN 978-1-4488-7928-1 (6-pack)
 1. Origami—Juvenile literature. 2. Fourth of July decorations—Juvenile literature. I. Title.
 TT870.O953 2013
 736'.982—dc23

                              2012009645

Manufactured in the United States of America

CPSIA Compliance Information: Batch # B4S12PK: For Further Information contact Rosen Publishing, New York, New York at 1-800-237-9932

38888000189690

Contents

Origami in Action

You may not think it's possible to make a hot dog or a majestic bald eagle from a single sheet of paper. With the correct folds and creases, however, there's no end to what can be made using **origami**!

Origami is the ancient art of folding paper to make small models. One place it's been popular for hundreds of years is Japan. It even gets its name from the Japanese language. The word "ori" means "folding," and "kami" means "paper." Origami enthusiasts don't just make models. They also invent new ones. Some origami experts can even make moving models, such as birds with flapping wings!

This book will take you step-by-step through six fun origami projects inspired by Fourth of July celebrations. Just follow the instructions and you'll soon be folding a range of paper masterpieces!

4

Get Folding!

Before you get started on your Independence Day origami models, here are some tips.

Tip 1

Read all the instructions carefully and look at the pictures. Make sure you understand what's required before you begin a fold. Don't rush, but be patient. Work slowly and carefully.

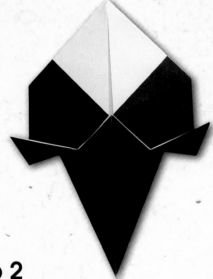

Tip 2

Folding a piece of paper sounds easy, but it can be tricky to get neat, accurate folds. The more you practice, the easier it becomes.

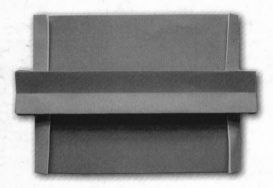

Tip 3

If an instruction says "crease," make the crease as flat as possible. The flatter the creases, the better the model. You can make a sharp crease by running a plastic ruler along the edge of the paper.

Tip 4

Sometimes, at first, your models may look a little crumpled. Don't give up! The more models you make, the better you will get at folding and creasing.

When it comes to origami, practice makes perfect!

Take a look at the models on this page. They have been made by experienced origami model makers. Keep practicing and you could soon be making complicated models like these!

Origami cactus

Modular origami is a type of origami in which lots of small, individual models, or units, are made, and then fitted together. This creates beautiful, complex sculptures.

Modular origami model

Some origami experts use a technique called wet-folding. They wet the paper so it can be molded to create smooth curves.

Have an Origami 4th!

The Fourth of July, officially known as Independence Day, **commemorates** July 4, 1776. That is the day the 13 original British colonies officially broke away from Great Britain to become the United States of America.

Actually, July 2, not July 4, was the day the leaders of the 13 colonies actually voted to separate from Great Britain. Some leaders thought July 2 would become the day of national **celebration**. But Congress officially approved the Declaration of Independence on July 4. That date quickly became America's national birthday, and to this day, saying "The 4th" says it all!

To make an origami 4TH, you will need:

3 sheets of origami paper

(Origami paper is sometimes colored on both sides or white on one side.)

STEP 1:
To make an origami 4, take a piece of paper and place it white side down. Fold along the dotted lines and crease.

STEP 2:
Unfold the creases, then fold in three of the corners so they don't quite meet in the center of the model, and crease.

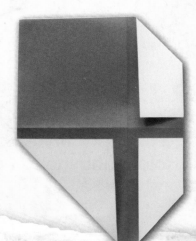

STEP 3:
Fold the right side behind the model along the dotted line, and crease.

STEP 4:
Fold back the bottom point behind the model along the dotted line, and crease.

STEP 6:
Finally fold back the point on the left behind the model, and crease. Your origami 4 is complete!

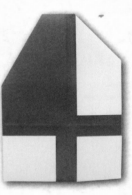

STEP 5:
Fold back the left side of the model along the dotted line, and crease.

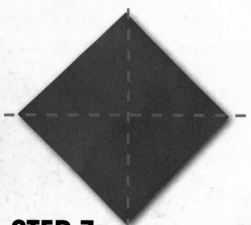

STEP 7:
To make an origami T, place a piece of paper white side down, fold along the dotted lines, and crease.

STEP 8:
Unfold the creases, then fold in the two sides so that they don't quite meet in the middle.

STEP 9:
Turn the model over. Fold down the top point, and crease.

STEP 10:
Fold up the bottom point, and crease.

STEP 11:
Now fold in the two sides, and crease.

STEP 12:
Turn the model over and your origami T is complete!

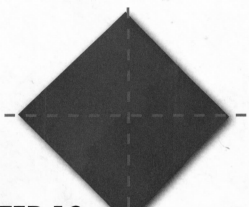

STEP 13:
To make an origami H, place a piece of paper white side down, fold along the dotted lines, and crease.

STEP 14:
Unfold the creases you made, then fold the top and bottom points so they meet in the center, and crease.

STEP 15:
Fold the two side points behind the model so they meet in the center, and crease.

STEP 16:
Tuck the two center points under and crease. Your origami H is complete!

Super Stars

Since 1777, the American flag has always had red and white stripes, white stars, and a blue field. The 13 stripes represent the original 13 colonies. The stars represent the States. In 1959, Hawaii became the fiftieth state, and our current flag, with 50 stars, was flown for the first time in 1960. The blue field, called a "union," stands for the United States as the Union, which is another name for the nation. Early leaders who approved the flag's design also chose stars to **symbolize** the nation as a new **constellation** taking its place in the heavens.

With this simple origami project, you can make your own constellation of stars for the Fourth!

To make origami stars, you will need:

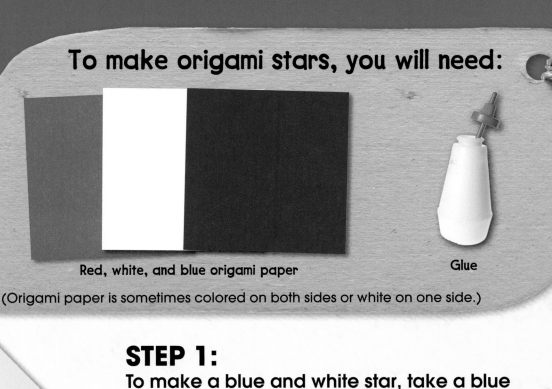

Red, white, and blue origami paper

Glue

(Origami paper is sometimes colored on both sides or white on one side.)

STEP 1:
To make a blue and white star, take a blue piece of paper and place it white side down. Fold in half diagonally, and crease.

STEP 2:
Now fold point A back on itself along the dotted line, and crease.

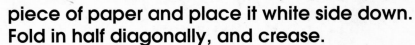

A

STONY CREEK LIBRARY
1350 GREENFIELD PIKE
NOBLESVILLE, IN 46060

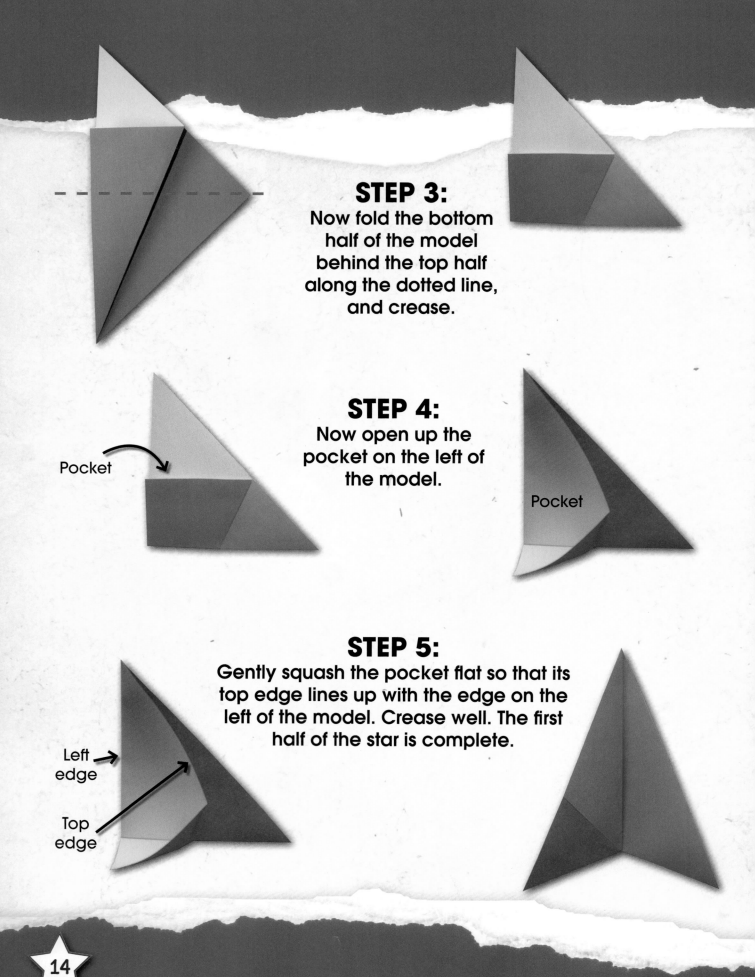

STEP 3:

Now fold the bottom half of the model behind the top half along the dotted line, and crease.

STEP 4:

Now open up the pocket on the left of the model.

Pocket

Pocket

STEP 5:

Gently squash the pocket flat so that its top edge lines up with the edge on the left of the model. Crease well. The first half of the star is complete.

Left edge

Top edge

STEP 6:

To make the second half of the star, take a white sheet of paper, fold it in half diagonally, and crease.

STEP 7:

Then fold the triangle in half again, and crease. The second half of the star is complete.

STEP 8:

Now slide the triangular second half of the star inside the first half and glue them together. Your star is finished!

STEP 9:

Mix up sheets of blue, red, and white paper to make different combinations.

Origami Bald Eagle

The bald eagle became a national US symbol in 1782. Early US leaders chose it because it had once been a symbol of the ancient Roman Republic, which, like the United States, was founded when a **revolution** replaced the king with elected officials.

The bald eagle gets its name from an older use of "bald" that means "streaked with white."

Here's a chance to use origami to make your own patriotic eagles!

To make an origami bald eagle, you will need:

A sheet of black origami paper

(Origami paper is sometimes colored on both sides or white on one side.)

STEP 1:
Place a piece of paper colored side down, fold along the dotted line, and crease.

STEP 2:
Unfold the creases, then fold two sides into the center, and crease.

STEP 3:
Fold the top point behind the model, and crease.

STEP 4:
Fold the two sides behind the model along the dotted lines, and crease. Then unfold again.

Diamond shape

Your model
should look
like this.

STEP 5:
Now lift up point A. Gently fold and squash the paper
down so it creates a diamond shape, and crease well.

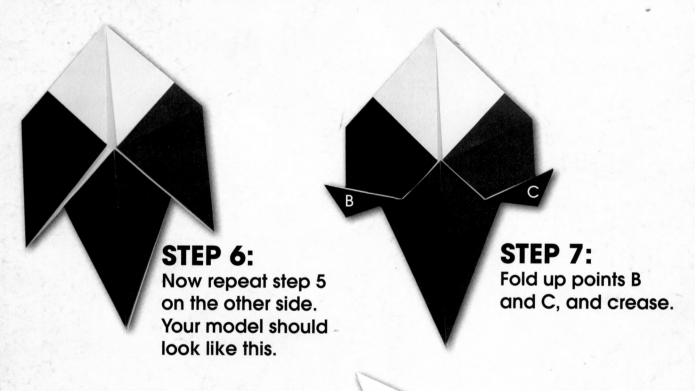

STEP 6:
Now repeat step 5
on the other side.
Your model should
look like this.

STEP 7:
Fold up points B
and C, and crease.

STEP 8:
Now close up the model along
its center fold. The model should
look like this.

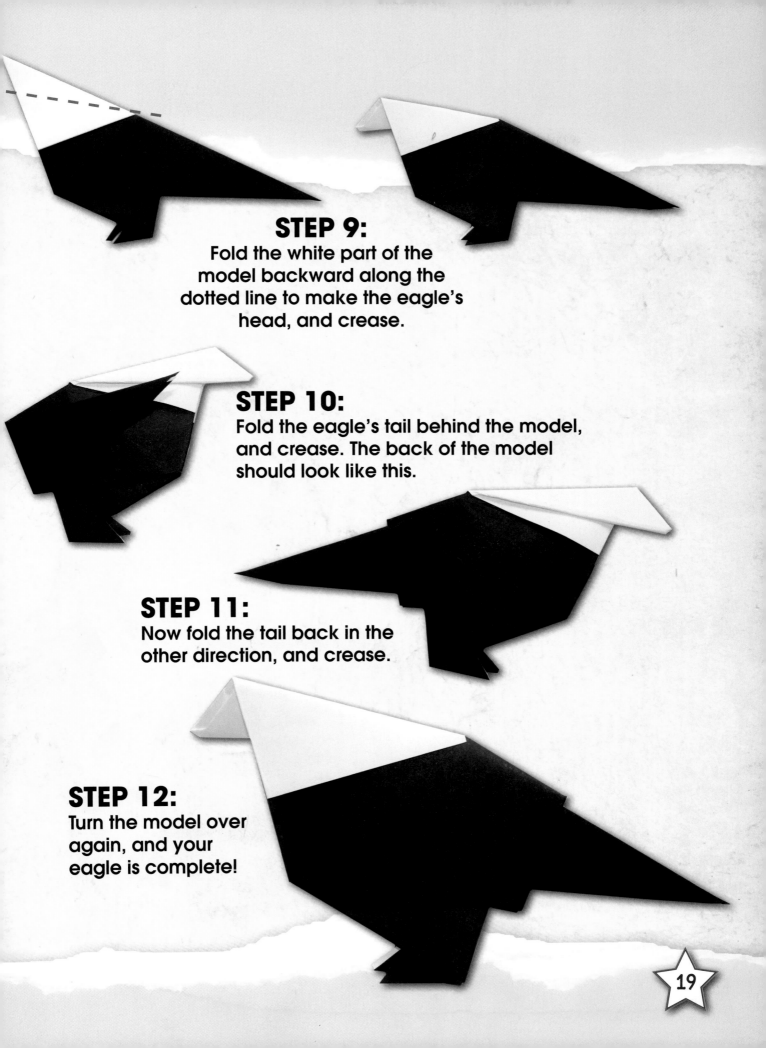

STEP 9:
Fold the white part of the model backward along the dotted line to make the eagle's head, and crease.

STEP 10:
Fold the eagle's tail behind the model, and crease. The back of the model should look like this.

STEP 11:
Now fold the tail back in the other direction, and crease.

STEP 12:
Turn the model over again, and your eagle is complete!

Holiday Hot Dogs

One name for a hot dog, "frankfurter," tells us that it's a sausage from Frankfurt, Germany. To most Americans, however, hot dogs are totally American. Many people like to grill hamburgers and hot dogs at outdoor barbecues to celebrate the Fourth of July.

Here's how to make some fun origami hot dogs—or veggie dogs, if you prefer! You can decorate your holiday barbecue with them.

To make an origami hot dog, you will need:

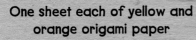

We've made this hot dog by folding with two sheets of paper (white sides touching). Use a small piece of double-sided tape to hold them together if you wish.

One sheet each of yellow and orange origami paper

(Origami paper is sometimes colored on both sides or white on one side.)

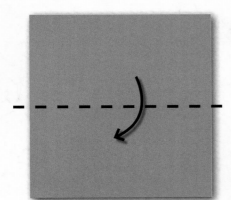

STEP 1:
Place the paper so the hot dog color is on top. Fold in half along the dotted line, and crease.

STEP 2:
Now fold the top flap back up along the dotted line, and crease.

STEP 3:
Now fold the top half of the model back down again along the dotted line, and crease. You will have created a pleat, or an accordion effect, in the center of the paper.

STEP 4:
Turn the model over and repeat steps 2 and 3 on the other side. Your model will then look like this.

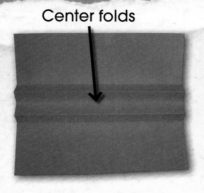

Center folds

Hot dog

STEP 5:
Open up the sheet of paper and you will see the accordion folds in the center. Squash them flat. You've just made the hot dog!

STEP 6:
Now turn the model over. Fold back the two corners to create small triangles, and crease. Then unfold again.

Hot dog flap

Small fold

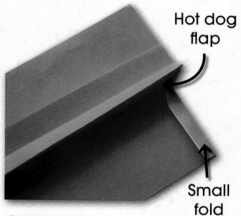

STEP 7:
Now turn the model over. Lift up one of the hot dog's flaps and make a small fold at the edge of the paper.

STEP 8:
Crease the fold and squash the hot dog flap back down. The small triangle fold you made in step 6 will help you make this move.

STEP 9:
Now repeat step 8 on the other side of the hot dog.

STEP 10:
Repeat steps 6 to 8 two more times until all four ends of the hot dog bun are folded in.

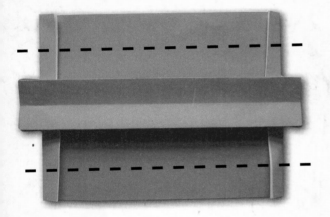

STEP 11:
Now fold the top half of the model down and the bottom half up along the dotted lines, and crease.

STEP 12:
Your hot dog will now be encased in its bun. Fold behind or scrunch under any pointed corners or sharp edges to give the hot dog and bun a more rounded shape.

Fireworks for the 4th

When American colonists first declared their independence, one of their leaders, John Adams, envisioned the anniversary of the nation's independence as a day of celebration. He predicted parades, games, shows, bells, speeches, and sports. He also envisioned "illuminations," which in his time probably meant fireworks.

Even that long ago, fireworks would have been a common way of celebrating special occasions. After all, they had been invented in China over a thousand years earlier!

Capture the sparkle and spirit of Fourth of July fireworks by making a display of multicolored origami starbursts.

To make an origami fireworks display, you will need:

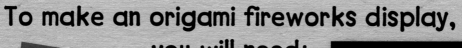

Scissors

Glue

A large piece of black cardboard

Sheets of origami paper in your favorite colors

(Origami paper is sometimes colored on both sides or white on one side.)

STEP 1:
Place the paper colored side down, fold up along the dotted line, and crease.

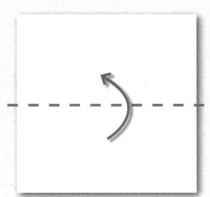

STEP 2:
Fold up along the dotted line, crease well, then unfold.

STEP 3:
Fold down along the dotted line, crease well, then unfold.

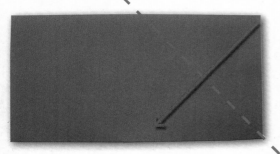

B

A

STEP 4:
Make a fold so that point A touches point B, and crease.

STEP 5:
Fold point C back along the dotted line, and crease.

STEP 6:
Fold point D up along the dotted line, and crease.

STEP 7:
Now fold the right side of the model behind the left side along the dotted line, and crease well.

STEP 8:
Now cut along the dotted line. Unfold the bottom part of the model. Your starburst is ready!

Unfold this half

STEP 9:
Make starbursts in lots of colors and glue them to a large piece of black cardboard!

Perfect Pinwheels

Everyone loves the swirl of colors and the sound that pinwheels make when they are attached to bicycles in Fourth of July parades. They are very simple little machines, and yet they are based on the same science we use to generate energy with wind power. So in a way, pinwheels are miniature windmills!

This project will give you a chance to make origami pinwheels that you can actually use to decorate your bike, house, or holiday cookout. You can also blow on them or hold them up to the wind and watch them spin.

To make pinwheels, you will need:

Origami paper in your favorite colors

Paper fasteners

Drinking straws

(Origami paper is sometimes colored on both sides or white on one side.)

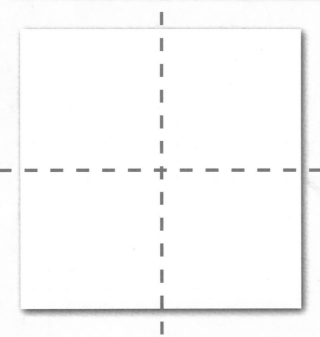

STEP 1:
Place the paper color side down, fold along the dotted lines, and crease.

STEP 2:
Unfold the creases, then fold the two sides into the center so they meet at the middle fold, and crease.

STEP 3:
Fold the top of the model down and the bottom up so they meet in the middle, and crease.

STEP 4:
Now open up the bottom fold and gently fold and squash the paper so it lies flat and creates two points. Crease hard.

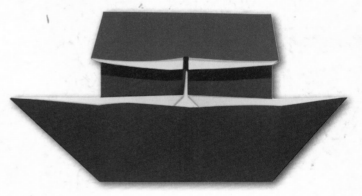

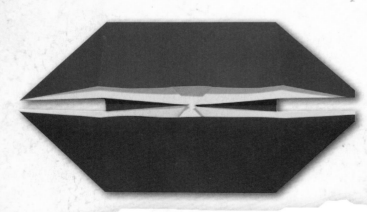

STEP 5:
Repeat on the other side of the model. Your model should now look like this.

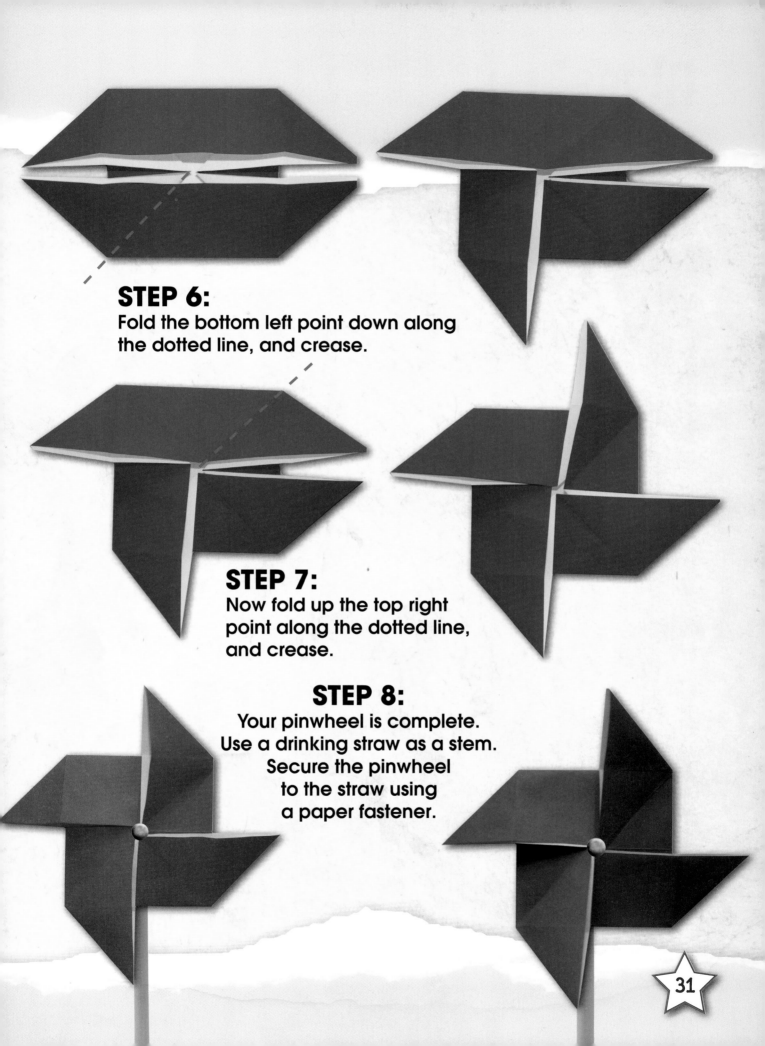

STEP 6:
Fold the bottom left point down along the dotted line, and crease.

STEP 7:
Now fold up the top right point along the dotted line, and crease.

STEP 8:
Your pinwheel is complete. Use a drinking straw as a stem. Secure the pinwheel to the straw using a paper fastener.

Glossary

celebration (seh-luh-BRAY-shun)
Observance of special times, with activities.

commemorates (kuh-MEH-muh-raytz)
Remembers and shows respect for a person or event.

constellation (kon-stuh-LAY-shun) A group of stars forming a pattern in the sky that can be recognized and named, usually after an animal or a famous figure from mythology.

origami (or-uh-GAH-mee) The art of folding paper into decorative shapes or objects.

revolution (reh-vuh-LOO-shun)
The overthrow, or the attempt to overthrow, usually by force, a government or some other ruling body in favor of something new.

symbolize (SIM-buh-lyz) To stand for or represent something else, such as an important event or person.

Index

Websites

Due to the changing nature of Internet links, PowerKids Press has developed an online list of websites related to the subject of this book. This site is updated regularly. Please use this link to access the list:
www.powerkidslinks.com/horig/inde/